G000150434

A FIVE-BALLOON MORNING

NEW MEXICO HAIKU

CHARLES TRUMBULL

RED MOUNTAIN PRESS
SANTA FE, N.M.

© 2013 Charles Trumbull

Cover image and design © Susan Gardner, 2013

Author's photograph © Susan Gardner, 2013, used by permission.

All rights reserved. No part of this book may be reproduced in any form, by any means, electronic or mechanical, without permission in writing from the author, except for brief quotations for the purpose of reviews.

ISBN 978-0-9855031-3-0
Printed in the United States of America

Second Printing

RED MOUNTAIN PRESS
Santa Fe, New Mexico
www.redmountainpress.us

A Five-Balloon Morning

New Mexico Haiku

for my father
who would have been 100 this year

NEW MEXICO & HAIKU

At first glance the American Southwest and a three-hundred-year-old Japanese poetic genre might seem to be an awkward pairing. Yet haiku seems to be the perfect medium to describe the physical and emotional beauties of New Mexico. Haiku are poems about nature, and our state certainly enjoys nature in abundance. The spareness of haiku diction echoes the vast spaces of, say, the Llano Estacado or the winter sky over Taos. Haiku are short, laconic, concrete—perfect for describing Shiprock or a kiva of the Ancients. Haiku rely on the juxtaposition of two concrete images for a sense of contrast or comparison, ideal for probing the interrelations among the Native, Hispanic, and European cultures of our state. Imagine haiku as a kaleidoscope of discrete bits and pieces—dewdrops, sparks, river stones, aspen leaves, fireflies, glass splinters, potsherds....

Without suggesting any direct connection or influence, one could also point out a historical parallel between Edo-Period Japan and the years of exploration and colonization in New Mexico. For example, Matsuo Bashō, the great pioneer of haiku, began his famous pilgrimage to the northern provinces of Japan in 1689; three years later, Diego de Vargas accomplished his *reconquista* of our area.

New Mexico has long been a hotbed of haiku: pioneers of the American haiku movement such as Foster Jewell, Elizabeth Searle Lamb, and

William J. Higginson all lived here. Hispanic haiku poets and scholars including Álvaro Cardona-Hine and Gary L. Brower make their homes in the state. Native Americans Gerald Vizenor and N. Scott Momaday have brought their haiku to New Mexicans.

My roots in New Mexico run deep: my grandfather hailed from a prominent Illinois political family and moved here in 1904. He married a granddaughter of the founder of the Browne & Manzanares mercantile firm of Las Vegas and Socorro. I grew up in Las Vegas, but left to go to college and lived elsewhere for 50 years before returning home in 2009. I discovered Japanese short verse in the book nook at Los Artesanos gallery on the Las Vegas plaza in the late 1950s but only began writing haiku in 1992. Now, as far as poetry goes, I can hardly write anything else!

A Five-Balloon Morning collects bits and pieces: my impressions from a small-town New Mexico childhood, my many visits home while I was living in the East and overseas, the joys and vicissitudes of living in northern New Mexico, an interlude about the momentous events of 1945, and a sentimental tour to various points around the state. Please sit back and join me in a kaleidoscopic look, through the lens of haiku, at the Land of Enchantment.

Charles Trumbull
Santa Fe, May 17, 2013

LEAVES FROM THE TREE

raking into piles
leaves from the tree
I climbed as a boy

whiff of creosote—
childhood summers
walking railroad ties

across the old bridge
I still find myself checking
for La Llorona

two boys
flip the stinkbug on its back
dog days of summer

trading for piñon nuts
I leave a silver trinket
for the pack rat

Cocker Spaniel hair
mars the perfection
of the cockle burr

                    faces
                    children make
                    carving pumpkins

           on the china shelf
           with the family Haviland
           her third-grader's pot

back-to-school week
underfoot the crunch
of sunflower shells

small-town high school
Dad's first girlfriend
teaches me history

click of the shutter
the whole family
exhales together

Philmont campout
too many extra stars
to find the constellations

sunrise
among the silent earth movers
a fawn

almost breakfast time—
fumbling in the coffee can
for a night crawler

jacklighting
a rustle in the bushes …
the rabbit dies

breast of dove
between my teeth
a bit of shot

line drive to center
all faces turn toward
the alfalfa field

stretching fence wire
now and then
the rasp of a locust

heading and heeling ...
a cowboy loses his hat
in the summer sun

breathless August heat
piñon wood stacked
up to the *vigas*

my parents' ashes strewn
on Johnson Mesa
wind stirs the aspens

first Christmas
without my mother
without my childhood

LEAVING NEW MEXICO
& COMING BACK HOME

departing at dawn
sun draws the mist
from the mountains

sunflower field
all the windmills
face the same way

Colfax County
the oncoming driver
tips his hat

east to Oklahoma
a pronghorn buck
greets my morning

the quiet of the cattle
in the feed yards
this overcast day

cloudless plains sky
my soul completely
exposed to God

oil rig not pumping   wild turkeys

after gassing up
I pass the same trucks
all over again

late-night diner
the clink of a spoon
on a stoneware mug

cheap motel
all night the cries
of mating frogs

spring break
mother welcomes me home
with a list of chores

hometown visit
fine sand in the doorways
of vacant storefronts

day lilies
push through the horse fence
first day of summer

class reunion
I struggle to recall
her married name

grass hill country
a boy rides bareback
over red earth

along a strand of barbed wire dewdrops

roadside vultures
barely flap their wings
U-Haul headed west

small-town café
a special tip for the waitress
named Destiny

rural speed limit sign   the necessary bullet hole

home again!
on the radio
a *ranchera*

A COYOTE CIRCLING

desert hours …
watching for the lilacs
to blossom again

aspens and chamisa
converge
on a shade of yellow

en la boca cerrada
no entran
flores de cereza

          in and out
                    of sunlight
          the magpie

   a towhee scratches
   in the underbrush
   my unquiet heart

   yucca in full bloom
   a sky full
   of cumulus clouds

wild asters
brilliant in the field
after the fire

a jay works the bank
of the eroded arroyo
autumn morning

cold rain on snow
a coyote
circles the garden

a strutting raven
on the parapet …
sifting snow

cold spell
a flicker sips at ice melt
in the *canale*

pale moon
through the pelvis of a mule
desert quietude

Hopi silversmith
teaches his son
to make a chain

potter's glaze
the soft purple cast
of her eyes

farmers market
the Indian corn seller's
snaggletoothed smile

peak of the season
a vendor's melon sample
crawling with wasps

cooling breeze
the supermarket sets up
the chile-roasting cage

heat lightning
the casino cashier's
liquid silver choker

triple sevens
his aluminum crutch
clatters to the floor

above her sun dress
the whiteness of her shoulders
pear blossoms

bait shop
that cute salesgirl
flirting

wind-twisted juniper
at the precipice
you take my hand

we both agree
not to speak about the past
whispers of cottonwoods

daydreaming
the cry of the elk
is me

taut strands
of barbed wire
so much left unsaid

that pile
of used adobe bricks
she won't change her mind

in the dark corner
where the crucifix hung
a white shadow

cathedral concert—
I mistake the tolling bells
for someone's ringtone

Christmas Muzak echoes in the empty mall stores

trash in the acequia
more than I wanted to know
about my neighbors

driveway
to the mobile home
stone lions

boulders fallen
from the sandstone cliffs
talk of family affairs

alone
with my Cheerios
and another missing child

fortune-teller's sign
Se Habla Español
would it be different?

full morning sun
the snowcap slides
off the *horno*

along the roadside
obscured by tumbleweeds
cluster of white crosses

two tapping canes
pass in the *alameda*
no words spoken

wind rising
a spring moon clears
the coyote fence

TRINITY

Human history changed in a flash on July 16, 1945, with the first explosion of an atomic bomb, which took place at the Trinity Site, a remote stretch of desert at the north end of the Jornada del Muerto ("Day's Journey of the Dead Man") in the Tularosa Basin east of Socorro, N.M. Located on the territory of White Sands Missile Range, the Trinity Site is closed to the public all but two days a year. Driving to the site proper, we pass through a guarded main gate and proceed several miles south. About an acre of land around ground zero, simply a three-foot-deep declivity with a small basalt obelisk marking the spot, is cordoned off with chain-link fencing. Photographs from 1944–45 are hung museum-style along the fence.

The McDonald Ranch, about three-quarters of a mile from ground zero, served as the headquarters and observation point for the scientists from Los Alamos who developed the atomic device. On display in the ranch house is a facsimile of Albert Einstein's letter of Aug. 2, 1939 to Pres. Franklin D. Roosevelt advising him of the scientific feasibility of making an atomic bomb and warning him of a growing interest in the development of uranium in Nazi Germany. A model of "Fat Man," the bomb dropped on Nagasaki, is on display at the Trinity Site. (The first bomb, "Little Boy," was detonated over Hiroshima.) Trinitite is the name given to the green glass-like mineral fused from sand by the intense heat of the atomic blast.

Sixty-five-plus years on, we contemplate how this event, the apotheosis of modern science, instantaneously shifted the political, economic, military, and especially moral landscape of the modern world. J. Robert Oppenheimer, chief scientist on the Manhattan Project, famously quoted a line from the *Bhagavad Gita:* "Now I am become Death, the destroyer of worlds."

This haiku sequence records, journal-style, impressions from a visit to the Trinity Site in October 2011.

October dawn
a fireball rises
over the mountain

Jornada del Muerto
autumn morning haze
fills the valley

looking for antelope
along the roadside
DANGER signs

Trinity Site
in the guard's vehicle
fuzzy dice

we drive through the gate
feeling very American—
weeds through asphalt

small talk
"my father
was at Oak Ridge ..."

squabbling children—
the grasshopper
hops away

ground zero
we walk into a depression
decades old

black lava obelisk
like a tombstone
marks the spot

everyone wonders
about lingering radiation—
rattle of a locust

65 years:
the persistence
of trinitite

scraping the dirt
with my toe—
a grain of green glass

Trinity's garden:
snakeweed, Russian thistle,
yucca, sagebrush

Porta Potty
someone has scrawled
"Army"

visitors gawk
at souvenir mugs, hats, T-shirts, …
Fat Man

the Stars and Stripes stretched tight across a tourist's breasts

McDonald Ranch silence shattered by two sonic booms

"clean room"
at the ranch house
the Einstein letter

empty magpie nest in a mesquite bush

we leave the site
in the *malpaís*
sand shifts slowly

TURTLE DANCE

from Santa Fe to Taos the Milky Way

rhythms of the Turtle Dance
beneath Taos Mountain
first dawn

remaining snow
a bald eagle soars
over the Rio Grande

the leader of our bird walk
says he's going deaf
wind in the tall pines

bend in the trail
a juniper branch
worn smooth

mountain lilac
the adobe church
at Las Trampas

cliffs of Bandelier
a wisp of juniper smoke
from down the canyon

ponderosa pines
reaching to the cliff tops
winds of the ancients

Ghost Ranch
the silent passage
of a crow

box canyon
echoes of swallows
box canyon

conjunto music
blaring from dusty low-riders
Española summer

                        sandstone formation
                        an old Navajo woman
                        bends into the wind

                                                Chimayó shrine
                                                plenty of parking
                                                for the handicapped

on the bronze pate
of Saint Francis of Assisi
pigeons

tourist season
up and down Canyon Road
cottonwood fluff

October sun
the Zuñi jewelry seller
huddles in her blanket

pierced Chicago punk eye to eye with the Tewa silversmith

cracking adobe
and a rough wooden cross
Cochiti drumbeats

ancient lava flow
a small *descanso* nestles
among the rocks

sunrise
over the Sandias—
a five-balloon morning!

bosque fire
heavy smoke covers
the factory district

Very Large Array
the news on NPR seems
very far away

small-town directions
all start at
McDonald's

Little Texas—
next to his 6-inch belt buckle
the rancher's iPhone

Bible Belt town
the second largest building
the Second Baptist Church

dust devils
whirl past
a Pentecostal church

Roswell gas station
two goths ask the way
to the UFO site

Carlsbad Caverns
tourists flock to see
the bat flight

beyond the Pecos—
a white horse grazes
in the bottomland

Tucumcari dawn
I thought I saw the ghost
of old Tom Joad

weed-choked ruts
of the Santa Fe Trail
cross the barbed wire

moon over Clayton
tonight there's only me
and a radio preacher

CREDITS

These haiku have been published previously, often in slightly different versions:

"across the old bridge" — Trumbull, *Narrow Footbridge* [broadsheet], 2007

"after gassing up" — *South by Southeast* 6:3 (1999)

"alone" — *The Heron's Nest* 5:5 (May 2003)

"along a strand" — Trumbull, "Fever Dream" [haibun], *Frogpond* 34:2 (spring/summer 2011)

"along the roadside" — *Tinywords* [Internet], April 18, 2003

"aspens and chamisa" — Odes and Offerings [ekphrastic art project], Santa Fe Community Center Gallery, May–June 2012; artwork by Donna Rutt

"beyond the Pecos" — Jim Applegate, ed., *Small Canyons 5 Anthology* (2010)

"click of the shutter" — *Acorn* 4 (spring 2000)

"cold rain on snow" — an'ya and Peter B., eds., *In Pine Shade* (HSA Members' Anthology 2011)

"day lilies" — *Acorn* 5 (fall 2000)

"desert hours" and "wild asters" — "Two for Marian Olson," Trumbull, *The Orb Weaver's Web* [broadsheet], 2010

"east to Oklahoma," "roadside vultures," and "Tucumcari dawn" — Jim Applegate, ed., *Small Canyons 4 Anthology* (2009)

"*en la boca cerrada*," "remaining snow," and "sunrise over the Sandias" — Scott Wiggerman and Constance Campbell, eds., *Lifting the Sky: Southwestern Haiku & Haiga* (Dos Gatos Press, 2013)

"Ghost Ranch" — AxleArt Haiku Roadsign Project, week 14 (Santa Fe, Aug. 30–Sept. 5, 2011)

"late-night diner" — Trumbull, *The Snowman's Companion* [broadsheet], 2009

"line drive to center" — *The Heron's Nest* 3:1 (January 2001)

"moon over Clayton" — *Tinywords* [Internet] 11:3 (Jan. 2, 2012)

"oil rig not pumping," "the quiet of the cattle," and "weed-choked ruts" — Jim Applegate, ed., *Small Canyons 7 Anthology* (2012)

"spring break" — Garry Gay, ed., *Light and Shadow* (HSA Members' Anthology 1998)

"stretching fence wire" — *Bottle Rockets* 3:2 (#6, spring/summer 2002)

"sunflower field" — Michael Dylan Welch and Grant Savage, eds., *Into Our Words* (Haiku North America Anthology 2009)

"sunrise / among the silent earth movers" — *The Heron's Nest* 2:8 (August 2000)

"taut strands" — *Modern Haiku* 40:3 (autumn 2009)

"the leader of our bird walk" — Trumbull, *The Orb Weaver's Web* [broadsheet], 2010

"Trinity" — *Frogpond* 35:3 (autumn 2012)

"two boys" — Trumbull, *Bugs* (Haiku Canada Sheet, 2006)

"we both agree" and "wind-twisted juniper" — Trumbull, "Moonlight on a White Iris" [sequence], *New Mexico Poetry Review* 4 (2011)

"wind rising" — Trumbull, *Transit of Venus* [broadsheet], 2012